Stuffie Summer: One Man Eats Every Stuffed Quahog In Rhode Island (And He's Not Clamming Up About It)

DAVID NORTON STONE

Copyright © 2013 David Norton Stone

All rights reserved.

Cover photograph by Josh Stone

ISBN: 0985493976
ISBN-13: 978-0985493974

To my grandfather, Earl Francis Martin, who gave me
my first typewriter and always encouraged me to write.

It is July 21, midway through my Stuffie Summer, and I am at the Warren Quahog Festival at Burr's Hill Park speaking with a man who has such a high tolerance for heat that I surmise he must have dragon's blood coursing through his veins. Not that Rick, who bakes the stuffies, hasn't taken precautions. He has wrapped a wet towel around his neck, tucking the ends under the collar of his black, sleeveless t-shirt. "This is my cool towel,"

Rick says. His hands and forearms are protected by silver quilted mitts. The skin on the only exposed parts of his body, the arms between elbows and shoulders, is red, but not alarmingly so. There isn't a stain on his white apron.

At the Warren Quahog Festival I have seen a man combine half a gallon of chopped clams with five pounds of batter and mix it with a cement mixer fitted with a dough hook. I have seen a woman in a red gingham apron pile strawberries on shortcakes the size of throw pillows and sell them for $5.00. I myself have exchanged a fin for a strawberry shortcake and over an hour later have been made aware by sign language that I have whipped cream evidence thereof somewhere on my cheek. I have seen a large float depicting Warren, Rhode Island with a banner that says "Small Town America Where Independence Lives." The float is so detailed that it includes a life size seagull in a seagull's nest, prompting me to wonder why I have never seen a real seagull in a nest. Small Town America Where Seagulls Nest. I have seen flags flown at half staff by order of the President in respect for the victims of a shooting in Aurora, Colorado the day before. I have sat on the grass in front of a bandshell with my fellow citizens, who are somewhat more subdued than usual that day. I have watched a man use a clam knife to open cherrystones and littlenecks faster than the eye can see and listened to him say, incorrectly, that quahogs are found only in Rhode

Island. They exist elsewhere, but the best tasting ones come from here, so his puffery is forgivable. I have seen a lot this day, but nothing like Rick.

His sunglasses have slid almost to the end of his nose, so maybe there is a hint of perspiration on his face, not that I can see it. He is about to open the door of the restaurant-size Blodgett oven that stands on the grass under the tent, having just explained to me that the temperature inside the oven is 450 degrees. It has a gas flame and a fan that circulates the heat. Rick has had professional restaurant experience and has used an oven like this to cook bacon. It is clear he respects the Blodgett.

Other years when he has cooked the stuffies at this festival the temperature has been in the high nineties with humidity at one hundred percent, and it has felt cooler inside the oven than out. Today, though, the temperature is in the low eighties with seventy percent humidity. But you wouldn't know that here where the stuffies get made. Rick opens the Blodgett. I whisper an amen.

*

"How hot was it?" you ask about my Stuffie Summer.

Stuffie not stuffy, although it got pretty toasty by the Blodgett at the Warren Quahog Festival, which I'll return to in time. I'm talking about stuffed quahogs. My Stuffie Summer was a season stuffed with lots of big quahog shells, overstuffed themselves with a stuffing of chopped quahogs, breading, onion and celery, and baked. Stuffies are served hot, and sometimes they are made even hotter by the incorporation of Portuguese chourico into the stuffing, or a couple of shakes of hot sauce on top.

What prompted me to eat every stuffed quahog in New England in one summer? No one has written exclusively about stuffies before, despite their popularity and ubiquity in Rhode Island, and I like being a pioneer. I find that the best way to learn about anything is to stuff yourself with it. I had embarked on a similar quest the summer before with clamcakes and wrote about it in my book *Clamcake Summer: One Man Eats Every Clamcake in Rhode Island (Or Dies Frying)*. By eating a lot of the same delicious summer treat you stand to gain a lot of weight, but you also become aware of the subtle distinctions that separate the good from the great.

I find that the familiarity from repetition does not breed contempt or even boredom. During the week I work and live in New York City, returning to Rhode Island each weekend. I bought an old house, my getaway, in my hometown of Warwick six years ago. My Stuffie Summer was a kind of frustrating sweaty-palmed unconsummated summer romance, in which Saturday and Sunday's stuffie dates were over too soon and I found myself constantly looking forward to what was going to happen on the next date.

Stuffed things have an air of holiday celebration

about them. The stuffed turkey, the fruit stuffed pork loin, the piñata. Stuffies are no exception, I think, on my date with the inaugural stuffie of Stuffie Summer at Iggy's Doughboys & Chowder House, 889 Oakland Beach Avenue in Warwick.   The stuffed clam is served in a paper boat. A piece of lemon pierced by a plastic cocktail fork stands ready at the right of the container for a squirt of citrusy acid. Wedged between the shell and back of the paper boat is a packet of Red Devil Pepper Sauce, daring me. The convex mound of the stuffing completes the clam again, stands in for the half of the shell that has been removed.

If you've ever steamed open your own quahogs, you were probably surprised at how small the clam is that hides within the heat opened shell. But here is plenty made from little. The addition of bread crumbs, onion, celery and butter to the clam has stretched a morsel of meat into a meal.

The sprinkling of paprika and parsley onto the top adds to the festive nature of the stuffie, as does the novelty of eating out of the shell. The stuffie is at once the food itself, the vessel in which the food is cooked and the serving dish on which it is served. How's that for easy cleanup? No pans to scrub or dishes to wash. You just throw away the shell when you're done. Or re-purpose it as an ashtray.

It is still spring, my bridal's veil is in bloom, but bathing suit season will be here soon enough. I have lost some weight over the winter (see

Clamcake Summer for the reason why I needed to lose weight) and I am undertaking this food odyssey with some trepidation. Will eating all these stuffies undo my success? Here's where the cocktail fork makes an appearance.

The tiny cocktail fork is as intrinsic to the eating of stuffies as the lemon and the hot sauce. When I was a teenage busboy at the Cowesett Inn in West Warwick, the commonplace cutlery was stored in plastic bins on a shelf at knee level, but the cocktail forks had a special place on the counter. I think we used them for the shrimp cocktail too, but it was for the stuffies that those little forks needed to be kept close at hand.

Of course those little trident tines are perfect for

pressing into a lemon wedge, but the small size also makes it easier to excavate the crunchy bits of baked stuffing from a rounded shell. A stuffie is after all a food served in a bowl (the shell) and a big fork is useless on that kind of slope. The cocktail fork is much handier.

The little fork is also to be the preserver of my weight loss. To take the measure of a stuffie, I don't need to eat the whole thing. One tiny bite from that little fork, at most two, should give me all the necessary flavor and information.

At Iggy's I bypass the lemon and hot sauce for one unadorned taste. Miniscule fork enters giant stuffie and….

Approximately twenty tiny forkfuls later I am staring

at my reflection in a scraped clean quahog shell. It's not going to be easy to stop after a few bites. There's such variation in each bite. Sometimes I taste a lot of clam, sometimes it's the vegetables that predominate. Bites from the top are buttery crunchy. I think of this crust as the clam skin. And then I have to see how the stuffing changes quality when doused with hot sauce. Each stuffie, I am actually not too disappointed to announce, is going to require more than a couple of tiny forkfuls to appreciate.

This gives me the idea for the rating system for this quest. The best stuffies are deserving of a twenty cocktail fork rating, because one or two forkfuls isn't enough. In the case of these special stuffies, I can't stop eating them until the shell is empty (sometimes even two shells). All the stuffies I write about here have earned twenty cocktail forks.

*

Unlike most other clam shack treats, stuffies aren't cooked out in the open. Stuffing them is done in private. This makes it a little harder than with other foods to determine what's in them or if they are even made on the premises. I learn pretty quickly that the question, "Are your stuffies homemade?" is often an awkward one. A few places haughtily assure me that everything they serve is made there. But the best places not only tell me who makes them, but send him or her out from the kitchen to chat.

I gravitate to places that boast in their menu that their stuffies are homemade or whose ingredients are so unique they have to be bespoke. I also survey friends about their favorite stuffies. "You'd have to go to Fall River. They make them best there," says a man born in Fall River. Someone else specifies the Crow's Nest in Warwick. She can't explain why, she has just always enjoyed them there. "My mother makes them best," a teacher friend confides. But more often with stuffies, people like most of them equally as long as the cooks don't tamper too much with the basic recipe. "Yup they messed it up. Chefs are such show offs," one friend sniffed at a stuffie that had the temerity to contain sausage. Despite this conservatism I can think of few foods so easily adaptable to improvisation as the stuffie, and I welcome variety in my tastings. To lift a cocktail fork twenty times I have to be intrigued.

*

I have no idea where my stuffie search will lead me in Newport this fresh May day. I decide to let the locals do the work for me, stopping at the market that sells fresh fish and lobster at the end of the wharf to ask one of the old salts where I can find a good homemade stuffie. A typical talkative Yankee, he points to a restaurant right on the wharf.

I land at The Landing at 30 Bowen's Wharf in Newport. I ask the friendly, young hostess if they have good stuffies.

"Are you an expert or something?" she challenges.

Don't you love it when people answer a question with a question? I reply gamely with another question. "Can you just tell me if they are made here?"

She disappears into the kitchen and returns in a minute with the good news that their stuffies are indeed housemade. It's sunny enough to eat outside at the dockside bar with views of yachts and Goat Island, but I keep my jacket on. Burgees on sailboat masts snap and flap in the breeze, providing the correct sound effects for a stuffie tasting. A pair of stuffies arrive. Visually, I am intrigued by the bits of diced green pepper that stud the stuffing. That's already a little different. I take a bite and inventory what I expect to taste. Rich moist stuffing (check), tender clam (check), soft, sweet green pepper (check), onion and celery (check). But this stuffie has a kick to it. That didn't take long. Second stuffie of the summer, and I've landed in the chourico (pronounced by some as sha-deez, although most people don't pronounce the "r" as a "d").

Chourico is a Portuguese sausage made of pork, paprika, garlic, salt, pepper and vinegar or Portuguese red wine. It has a kick, and pairs well with clams. While some places will offer two choices of stuffies (mild and spicy), so popular is the chourico version that in many restaurants there is only one stuffie on the menu and it has chourico.

There is a large Portuguese population in Rhode Island, as well as in Fall River and New Bedford in Massachusetts (my maternal great grandmother was one hundred percent Portuguese). But it's not only ancestry that has made the stuffie a colony of Portugal. Chourico tastes good.

The stuffie at The Landing is full of chourico pieces, and the vegetables have been cooked in the rendered fat from the sausage. At this moment, I think the legislature should mandate that stuffies always include chourico.

My swoons have attracted the attention of management. Soon the chef Will comes out to talk to me, and I cajole him into divulging the recipe for my research. He brings it to me handwritten on a piece of ruled notepaper.

I won't divulge it here, because I prefer instead to encourage you to visit The Landing. Besides, I don't want to be responsible for a recipe that includes the ingredients "5 # Ritz crackers crushed" and "1 # butter." All this richness, plus some garlic and cayenne pepper, to surround "15 quahogs cooked and minced." And yet the clams themselves were never overshadowed. I walked off 1 # afterwards by strolling down Thames Street, looking at menus to see how many places featured stuffies (not many). I was surprised to see that wealthy Newport is a little stuffy to stuffies, as it is to clamcakes. Which reminds me that the chef at The Landing told me that he also serves clamcakes once the season gets going. What does he put in them? Chourico of course.

*

Just how popular are stuffies? My best friend for almost thirty years, a native Rhode Islander who can complete my sentences when the subject is clamcakes, confides to me over dinner in Provincetown, where he now lives, that he has never eaten a stuffie. Quite possibly he has never even seen one. Somehow our friendship survives this revelation.

The president of the *Clamcake Summer* Florida fan club (ok, my aunt) tells me that while she really likes clamcakes, she loves stuffies. She maintains her post.

Let's get a non-native's opinion. My movie buddy from Connecticut, who likes to speak pirate, takes a vacation in Newport with her sister and brother in law, who are visiting from California. None of them has had clamcakes or stuffies before. They try both while they are there. They adore the clamcakes, but damn to the depths whatever man thought of stuffies. Maybe if they'd had a little more rum it would be a different story.

But many people are like me. They love stuffies and clamcakes equally and please don't ever ask us to choose between them.

*

Blount's Clam Shack and Soup Bar at 371 Richmond Street in Providence is slick. The staff wears t-shirts

that say CHWDR, and dropping those pesky vowels
is far from the only break with tradition on display
here. Blount's has dared to add a new chwdr to the
pantheon. Its Clambake Chowder purports to put a
clambake in a soup. This mainly entails adding corn
and chourico to the clams and potatoes in a clear
Rhode Island chowder. I also try the chourico
clamcakes alongside Blount's chourico stuffie. Are
you beginning to see a trend here? Stuffie Summer
is turning into chourico summer, and I'm not
complaining. The stuffie has a delicate panko
stuffing and the clamcakes with their cornmeal
batter verge into hushpuppy territory. I speak to
the chef, David, who explains that he invented
chourico clamcakes in response to customer

demand when he worked at the Blount Clam Shack and Company Store in Fall River. It was a simple matter of replacing half the clams with chourico in deference to Fall River's love affair with chourico. Chourico has already conquered the stuffie, and I predict that the clams in clamcakes are going to start feeling crowded in the coming year thanks to chefs like David and Will. Blount's also has clam shacks in Warren and at Crescent Park, in addition to operating Blount Fine Foods World Headquarters of Clam Chowder in Warren. From the self proclaimed world headquarters of stuffies (my front porch), I salute Blount for perservering since 1880 and for shaking up the clam shack.

*

It was frustrating to try to trace the history of the stuffie. How can something have taken over the Rhode Island appetizer world but seemingly have come from nowhere?

The National Cook Book by Marion Harland (Charles Scribner's Sons, New York: 1896) contains a recipe for baked clams: "Open as directed at the head of this article, but be careful to reserve to every shell all the juice that belongs to it. Leave the clams in the lower shells, put a bit of butter, a drop of onion juice, and a sprinkle of paprica or cayenne, with a mere dust of salt upon each; replace the top shell, tying it on with a bit of cotton string; arrange the shells upon a hot pan and bake fifteen or eighteen minutes, according to the size of the clams. Remove the upper shells, squeeze upon each clam a few drops of lemon and the same of tomato catsup, and serve on the shells." While I like that trick of tying the upper shell back on, this wonderful recipe for baked clams is lacking one crucial thing to make it a stuffie: stuffing, and more than a "mere dust" of it.

Olive Green's *How to Cook Shell-Fish* (G.P. Putnam's Sons, New York: 1907) contains "One Hundred and Thirty Ways to Cook Clams." Stuffies aren't one of them. What about recipe 131, Olive? Did you not have room for stuffed quahogs? She does have a terse recipe for stuffed clams that's pretty similar, although it isn't expressly for quahogs. "Open, drain and chop two dozen clams. Mix with one cupful of cracker crumbs, one half cupful of hot milk, one quarter of a cupful of clam juice, two eggs well beaten, a heaping tablespoonful of butter and salt, and red pepper to season. Butter a dozen clam shells, fill with the mixture, sprinkle with crumbs, dot with butter, and bake until brown."

Dainty Dishes by Adolphe Mayer just can't contain a stuffie recipe. The stuffie shops at the Big & Tall Shop. It's husky not dainty. But, promisingly, there is a recipe for "Clams Farcis – Stuffed Clams." Mayer's recipe says: "Cut the belly part from 4 dozen large clams and chop up fine. Also chop fine 4 large shallots and fry them colorless in butter, then add the clams and cook them in their own juice; when boiling, add an equal amount of chopped mushrooms and 1 pint of thick Bechamel;

reduce to good consistency; and then bind with two or three egg yolks. Season to taste; put away to get cold. Fill some large well cleaned clam shells with the preparation. Strew over some bread crumbs, lay a small piece of butter on each clam, and brown in oven." J'adore Bechamel. However, this is not the stuffie I know.

The very old *Hotel St. Francis Cookbook* by Victor Hirtzler proposes a clam dish for those pesky leftover truffles: "Stuffed clams. Remove the clams from twenty four large Little Necks. Wash the shells very clean, so there will be no sand in them. Chop the clams, and mix with three fresh mushrooms chopped fine, one truffle, a little chopped parsley and three ounces of butter. Season with salt and pepper and then fill the shells. Place on a pan, sprinkle with grated cheese, put a small piece of butter on top of each, and bake in the oven for fifteen minutes. Serve on a napkin, with parsley, and lemons cut in half." But I've never seen a stuffie with mushrooms, let alone truffles, although both strike me as good ideas.

I thought I might find stuffies mentioned in the archives of old newspapers. A histrionic 1946 headline in the Providence Journal proves that clam adoration is nothing new in Rhode Island: "Wicked Blow Hits R.I. Epicures; Clambakes Curtailed Once Again." World War II was over, but the butter shortage remained, help was hard to find and the price of clams was up $4.00 per bushel over the prewar price. Some clambake operations weren't opening at all, and the ones that were opening had to do without buckwurst and serve clam broth in place of drawn butter. You can't make a good stuffie without butter, but stuffies don't even get a mention in the article, which is a wicked blow to me.

Newsflash! In 1954, Rhode Island Quahogs were added to the Army Master Menu. How exactly the Army planned to prepare them is not indicated by the quartermaster general, Major General K.L. Hastings. But I picture soldiers in mess halls around the country cautiously encountering their first stuffie.

In 1976, the Providence Journal reported about a

sea clam (not quahog) shortage and the consequent rise of all clam prices. There's discussion about the damage this was doing to Howard Johnson's trade in fried clam strips, but nothing at all about the effect on stuffie lovers.

Not until 1988 does the stuffie make headlines. On August 29, 1988 the Providence Journal reports "30,000 stuffies save day at Quahog Fest." It is a report on the International Quahog Festival in Wickford. Somehow or other 30,000 stuffies disappeared, but then were replaced after pleas for help to a local wholesaler. 30,000 stuffies had been sold the day before. The winner in the amateur category for best stuffie tied his clam closed with string to keep in moisture, Marion Harland's suggestion from 1896. The winner of the professional category was a sixteen year old young woman from the Broiler Bar and Grill who added red and green peppers and...can you guess?...chourico! She sure had her finger on the pulse of what was to come.

*

Aunt Carrie's has only reopened for the season a few weeks ago, but I can't believe I've delayed even this long to visit the Vatican of the clamcake located 1240 Ocean Road, Narragansett, Rhode Island. Their stuffies don't have the same renown as their clamcakes, but maybe I can help with that. The stuffies here have a spectacularly crunchy surface. My tastebuds tell me that the stuffing is made with bread crumbs that come from Aunt Carrie's homemade bread. The moist interior has a mayonnaise-smooth creaminess. To call it a plain stuffing sounds like a putdown, which is the furthest thing from my intent. It's plain in the way of an Aaron Copland Shaker hymn. And if simple pleasures aren't your thing, the stuffies here come with a side of cocktail sauce, which is itself an anomaly. A bottle of hot sauce would somehow be an anachronism in a place like Aunt Carrie's, so in tune with the timeless pleasures of the Rhode Island shore, as comfortable and quaint as the vintage oven that belonged to Aunt Carrie herself on display in the gift shop across the street. I go home with a loaf of homemade cinnamon raisin bread. The owner, Elsie, suggests I try heating a slice on a cast iron skillet. She also offers to give me the recipe for her French toast made with the bread. I tell her I'll get the recipe for that next time. When it comes to Aunt Carrie's there will always be a next time, and I look forward to celebrating its one hundredth birthday in 2020 with a candle stuffed clamcake.

*

My maternal grandfather, Earl Martin, loved stuffies. He also loved the beach. Correction, not the beach. He loved to be by the water. Every weekend in the summer, he drove his four daughters to Scarborough Beach, left them with their friends at their spot in front of the concession stand, and went off with his Sunday newspaper to the rocks in Galilee. The girls demanded at least four hours of baby oil basting time, so he had plenty of time to punctuate his reading with white chowder, clamcakes and a stuffie from the George's takeout window.

Afterwards, he would sometimes take the girls clamming at their favorite place next to the Escape Road. My mother remembers cutting her feet if she didn't want to get her sneakers wet. But bare feet were better for feeling the clams in the sand. Each girl was accessorized with a small clamming rake and a pail, as well as the best summer garb Gladdings department store had to offer. Earl supervised from the shore. The girls returned to Providence fragrant with eau de clam, and it was a battle for first bath in their one bathroom apartment, while their father cooked the clams.

Perhaps my grandfather's love for being near the water, but not in it, is owing to an act of heroism. During Hurricane Carol in 1954 he and his friend Eddie waded or swam into flooded areas around Sand Hill Cove to rescue people stranded there.

Or maybe he stayed out of the water because of his right arm. He couldn't lower it all the way. He could have been born that way, but the story he liked to tell is that he broke his arm too many times playing baseball. He attended every high school in Providence, being thrown out of each, and finally graduated at the age of 20 from Hope High School. He cut a dashing figure in the city, with a great head of hair (not inherited by me), a debonair Clark Gable mustache, and a Jack Benny dry wit. He was cagy about what he did for work in his twenties, but liked to hang around the posh Biltmore Hotel. At the advanced age of thirty he finally wed, but he never settled down.

Everyone he ever met adored him. Except, unfortunately, his wife, who only ever referred to him as "Mr. Martin." Mr. Martin, despite all those beach drives, failed to renew his license for about twenty years. It wasn't a high priority for him. One day his wife told the police that if they wanted to catch a person who was driving without a valid license they should look for his plate number. When the police stopped him on Lenox Avenue, the police asked him to open the trunk. Inside they found five dead Christmas trees that Mrs. Martin had asked him to get rid of. Every winter he would remove the tree from the living room to the front porch and then finally in the summer put it in the trunk.

Needless to say, if he was a procrastinator and a little irresponsible in his younger days, this was all part of his charm. And it is thanks to him that this book exists. I am referring to the sense of humor, respect for grammar and love of a good story he imparted to his daughters and grandchildren. But also to the money he gave my mother every Friday, because she was a struggling single parent, and this allowance helped pay for my piano lessons, my brother's hockey expenses and, most importantly, a good restaurant meal every weekend. He paid her an allowance until she remarried when I was a freshman in high school. I have friends who can count on one hand the number of times they went to a restaurant for dinner as children. Thanks to Papa, I ate out at least once a week, becoming a connoisseur of Rhode Island's best restaurants.

I'm talking about Lums for roast beef sandwiches, the Greenwood Inn for hot turkey sandwiches, Cappelli's on Airport Road for veal vento (layers of veal, Italian ham, and cheese), the Crow's Nest for clamcakes and chowder, Caserta's for pizza and pigs in the blanket, and the Great House for prime rib. Papa would joke that half of what he gave my mother went to food at these restaurants. But we treated him sometimes to the Harborside on East Greenwich cove for the best seafood. Sometimes Papa took my brother and me out to breakfast at a place in Apponaug where I was introduced to the unforgettable experience of a grilled English muffin. But all his grandchildren liked it best when he made us the best bacon and eggs in the world.

Unfortunately, I don't have his stuffie recipe to hand down to posterity. But I do have something. He always cooked Sunday supper because Mrs. Martin waitressed weekends at the Driftwood Restaurant in Pawtuxet. His Sunday staple was a sandwich cooked under the broiler. It consisted of a piece of white bread, covered by a couple of slices of

American cheese, topped in turn by two slices of bacon arranged criss-cross fashion, and two slices of tomato, precisely placed between the bacon slices, allowing the meat to crisp perfectly. He made four at a time and each girl would eat two. I hereby posthumously dub this sandwich Earl's Stuffie Broiled Cheese.

Eat it with a sharp knife and a cocktail fork, to savor each bite.

*

At Cap'n Jack's restaurant (706 Succotash Road, Wakefield) I have dinner with a friend who grew up in Rhode Island and now lives in California. If the sight of the Dunkin' Donuts at Logan Airport is enough to bring him to his knees in gratitude, you can imagine what the first taste of Rhode Island seafood of each summer does to him. It is a pleasure to be with someone who loves his home so much, and who is so appreciative of its foods that although a Saturday night at the Los Angeles Philarmonic or in Palm Springs is an okay night out, his best Saturday nights are spent making johnnycakes and Indian Pudding. For someone who has been away so long nothing less than clamcakes, chowder AND stuffies is required. We eat outside on the porch which sits over the tidal flats and, as the setting sun illuminates each blade of spartina grass, we compete in our praise of the stuffies, which feature bits of bright red pepper alongside the celery and clam. A homecoming deserves two desserts. First there are heaping bowls of grapenut pudding crowned with whipped cream. Then giant white frosted cookies shaped like lobsters from the bakery case in front of the restaurant. I suppose you're wondering why the cookies aren't red. Lobsters only turn red after they're cooked of course. But maybe these cookies are once in a lifetime genetic anomalies like the rare orange lobsters that have been in the news lately. White lobsters are the rarest color of all, except at Cap'n Jacks.

*

The State Recipe

Have you ever noticed that the state of Rhode Island on a map looks a bit like an open quahog, with the West Bay resembling the lower valve and the East Bay the upper valve of a clam? Stuff East Bay and West Bay with chopped clam and crumbs. Bake 25 minutes at 375 degrees. Pass the lemon juice and hot sauce. Garnish with Block Island.

*

The Cowesett Inn, at 226 Cowesett Avenue in West Warwick, where I worked as a busboy in high school and tasted my first stuffie, still serves a terrific (and huge) stuffie, adding linguica these days, and with the biggest pieces of clams I encountered in my Stuffie Summer. Back in my busboy days, I used to dream about moving away and becoming somebody. Would I have believed then that, years later, I would live in New York City but return to

Rhode Island every weekend to eat stuffies?

*

In mid-June my cousin Scott hosts a family party at his house in Warwick. I offer to make and bring stuffies, but am shocked at his response.

"Already got that covered, cuz. How about bringing the ice again?"

"Who's bringing stuffies?" I ask, wounded.

"My neighbor. He knows you're writing about them and wants to know what you think."

"Well, that's ok then."

The chief problem with bringing stuffies to a party is how to serve them hot. It's much easier to do this when you're the neighbor of the host. Ed's stuffies look better than most of the ones you find in restaurants. As a home cook, he can be less inhibited by people's expectations of what a stuffie should be. The most distinctive feature of his visually are that they are covered with crisp diced bacon, like big clams casino. There is just enough sage in the stuffing to add earthiness to the otherwise aquatic flavor.

Since I liked his stuffies so much, he thinks I might also like his seafood chowder. He disappears into his kitchen and emerges with a cup of what looks like New England clam chowder, but is actually a seafood chowder with mussels and crab complementing the flavor of the clams. It is complex and delicious.

As if I weren't already impressed enough, he invites me to go sailing to taste the clamcakes he makes on his sailboat. I've always conjectured that the best clamcakes are those made in the open air. I can only speculate how good those made at sea will taste.

I am glad I didn't bring stuffies that would stand in competition to these. But Ed is humble about his accomplishment and tells me that his go to place for stuffies, is Smitty's Seafood Market. I realize I've been remiss. Of course no Stuffie Summer is complete without tasting the stuffed quahogs at the local seafood markets.

*

The first surprise at Smitty's Seafood Market, in a

handsome brick building at 641 Warwick Avenue in Warwick, is that they have three kinds of stuffies on display in their glass display case. There is the mild (or classic) for $2.49, the spicy (with chourico) also $2.49 and the gourmet (with shrimp, scallops and crab mixed in with the clam) for $2.99. All are made right on the premises. This is truly stuffie heaven.

I am most intrigued by the gourmet version. The owner, Kevin, tells me that he uses a Ritz stuffing for that one, with a touch of sherry. I can see what looks like a whole bay scallop peeking out. Unfortunately I can't taste them on the spot, but I take home one of each to cook in my own oven.

Each is delicious but the gourmet one is a meal all by itself. The pieces of shrimp, scallop and crab are almost enough to seduce me away from my love of quahogs, and the stuffing itself is as buttery and rich as that found in baked stuffed shrimp.

You can also get that stuffing baked into a crab at Smitty's. That would be great to impress guests, but for me a quahog shell is a much more beautiful vehicle for stuffing than a creature with claws. Besides crabs and starfish are among the quahog's natural predators.

*

A lot of people don't like to make their own stuffies, or even to heat fresh or frozen ones made by others, because there is a misconception that cooking them might make your house smell slightly. This is false. Cooking stuffies will make your house smell a *lot*. But in a good way. Just don't leave the shells hanging around too long.

*

I've been dying to tell you this, but it's taken me awhile to get to July. They do something really weird with stuffies in Massachusetts! And I don't just mean the way they pronounce the word quahog.

I am in one of my favorite cities in the world, New Bedford, Massachusetts, a place I love for its association with *Moby-Dick*, its Whaling Museum, its beautiful buildings erected from the wealth derived from whaling and for its continued vitality as a seaport. Usually, when I come to New Bedford I want scallops straight off the boats, but I must maintain my stuffie focus.

I am in New Bedford today for Summerfest. A friend of mine is the world's biggest Benoit Bourque fan. Benoit and his Quebecois music is a perennial fan favorite at Summerfest, especially among those with French Canadian heritage. My friend has been raving about the music and food at this festival for years, and has finally convinced me to come to New Bedford for something other than the *Moby-Dick* Marathon. I'm happy I came. The people of New Bedford want me here! It is apparent from the friendliness of shopkeepers and townspeople, but also from the free parking in a huge garage made available for festival goers. Try parking for free in Newport in July.

Benoit plays two sets, and I can honestly say I have never seen a performer give more of himself to an audience. He plays bones and accordion, he dances, he changes his clothes because his first outfit is soaked through, he's on his knees, he's straddling a bass, he's jamming with his box playing son Antoine, who promises to enthrall New Bedford for as long as his father.

Just watching Benoit makes me hungry. There's a promising food area of the festival and among the vendors I find Captain Clamcakes, but the good skipper doesn't serve stuffies. It doesn't take long to find a restaurant that does. At Freestone's City Grill at 41 William Street, right in the thick of the festival action, I have a choice of a mild or spicy stuffed quahog. The menu adds the pronunciation next to the name: "Ko-Hog." I proudly order a spicy "Qwa-Hawg." I don't tailor my pronunciation to fit the local fashions.

And here's what I've been burning to disclose. At Freestone's, and elsewhere in New Bedford, they serve quahogs with butter. I don't mean there's butter in the stuffies. They give you little butter pats to put on top, as if a stuffie were a baked potato. I haven't been able to determine how this practice developed, but it's a great idea. Perhaps it's a Quebecois practice brought here by Benoit. I spread butter on top of the moist stuffie and then work it through the whole with my fork, glazing the clams, chourice, onions and celery. If *Stuffie*

Summer accomplishes nothing else, I hope it encourages Rhode Islanders to pass the butter, along with the hot sauce, lemon and cocktail sauce, when they serve stuffies.

*

And now from the humor department:

"Did you hear the one about the Rhode Islander who went to a fancy seafood restaurant in New York?"

"I think so. Didn't he order chowder and it came out red?'

"No. This is a different story. This guy orders surf and turf and they bring him filet mignon and a lobster tail. 'Waiter, what is this?' he asks, indignant. 'Your surf and turf, sir.' 'But where I come from surf and turf is a stuffie and a saugie,' the Rhode Islander protests. 'I don't know what either of those is, sir,' the waiter apologizes.

"Well, the man worked up such an appetite describing stuffed quahogs and thick skinned saugie hot dogs to the waiter that he managed to eat most of his lobster and filet and left the restaurant feeling pretty happy. The waiter later received a gift from the man in the mail. The card said it was a bottle of 'Rhode Island Champagne.'"

"What kind of coffee syrup was it, Autocrat or Eclipse?"

"Aw, so you do know this story!"

*

I can see the top of the roof of McKinley's Authentic Irish Pub (1 Division Street, East Greenwich) from my kitchen window. It is situated between my house and Greenwich Cove. Rumors of the good food there had been reaching me for a couple of years, and still I never visited until Stuffie Summer. Mainly because to walk there directly from my house requires trespassing on the railroad tracks, which I am too sheepish to do, and I am too slowed down by clamcakes and stuffies to walk the long way down King Street and then along the waterfront.

There is nothing ambiguous about these stuffies: "Great RI Stuffies (Homemade)," says the menu. The standard order contains three stuffies, which is a lot even for me. The waitress tells me it's no problem to order only one. This is an authentic Irish pub with an Italian twist. A signed picture of Big Tony hangs next to a portrait of Michael Collins. I've been ordering a lot of spicy stuffies this summer, but this gets the prize for hottest stuffie. It also has a spice note that is absolutely unique and that is absolutely complementary. Fresh dill exudes sweetness and the green of the Irish countryside.

A twenty cocktail fork stuffie right outside my window? What is the penalty for trespassing on the railroad tracks?

*

That Irish pub with the Italian grub reminds me of my aunt's stuffies. She is Irish, but is famed for her stuffies made with Italian sausage, both hot and sweet, as well as garlic and basil. Here is her recipe which, in an act of characteristic generosity, she specifically gave to me to include here. They should be called Disappearing Stuffies, because they seem to be gone the second they emerge from the oven at any family party.

Neen's Stuffies

2 dozen quahogs—medium size

1 pound of sweet Italian sausage

1 pound of hot Italian sausage

1 small to medium onion chopped

A couple of cloves of garlic chopped

3 or 4 stalks of celery chopped

Fresh basil chopped

Fresh parsley chopped

1 package of Pepperidge Farms Italian stuffing

1. Steam quahogs until opened and save water.
2. Chop clams as small as possible.
3. In a deep frying pan, saute in olive oil: garlic, onion, celery, basil, parsley and Italian sausage, continuously chopping sausage until cooked through and in small pieces.
4. In a large bowl blend sausage mixture with stuffing mix.
5. Add clams.
6. Sprinkle of Tabasco sauce.
7. Sprinkle of Worcestershire sauce.

8. Add several cups of quahog water until quite moist and good consistency for stuffing.

9. Salt and pepper to taste.

10. Stuff the shells.

11. Sprinkle with paprika.

12. Bake at 350 degrees until hot throughout.

13. Makes approximately 36 to 38 stuffies.

Aunt Neen included a postscript. "P.S. There is no written or measured recipe—this is just how I remember my mother made them."

*

We're finally back at the Warren Quahog Festival. I lose five pounds in sweat when Rick opens the Blodgett oven door, but don't actually incinerate. He removes a cookie sheet which holds eighteen stuffies, crammed shell to shell, each one like a three inch coal cooked to 165 degrees. It's time for them to go in the second oven.

Oh, haven't I mentioned the second oven? The stuffies go into a Duke oven to hold them at 145 degrees until they get sold to customers at the festival.

Rick is smiling as he answers questions about how one person can pull off cooking thousands of stuffies outdoors, at a summer seafood festival. But I think the real question is why anyone would put himself through this. There's only one answer, and I should have known, given my previous experience with the fine people who put out the best food at fairs and festivals throughout Rhode Island.

He's a volunteer and he's working for a cause dear to his heart.

The Warren Quahog festival is run by the Warren Barrington Rotary Club. The festival raises a lot of money, which is then distributed to charitable organizations in the community. By volunteering, Rick assures that a portion of the proceeds, tied to the hours he puts in, will make it to an organization he designates.

The statistics are mind blowing. He'll cook 17 cases of 70 stuffies this weekend, which will also require two or three cases of lemons and a case of bottled hot sauce. The stuffies are Captain Carl's Pride brand. Rick also cooks the stuffed scallops, which are made by another company. I don't ask how many of those he makes. I don't want to embarrass the scallops.

I thank Rick for his information, and he encourages me to walk around and enjoy the sights of Warren, especially Maxwell House, the oldest brick dwelling in town, where they do hearth cooking in the restored original fireplace. I think I've had enough ovens for one day, thank you.

Unable to take the heat of the outdoor kitchen, I venture around to the other side of the tent to buy a stuffie. They are priced $3.00 for one, $5.00 for two. I sit under a tent at a communal table and cool off. The stuffie is delicious, full of clams, onion and celery and dusted with a tasty spice blend on top. Strangely, I begin to miss the heat. I go back to the tent and order a clam boil full of steamer clams, chourico, bockwurst and potatoes. I burn my fingers tearing open the net it is steamed in, but don't care. I have survived Vulcan's Forge.

*

I recently heard someone say, in the context of a food festival that was expected to attract Woodstock size crowds, that food is the new rock and roll. If this is true, then what is the rock equivalent of the stuffie? I conclude that the stuffie is like Adele, glamorous when she wants to be, but otherwise approachable, as well as soulful, blunt, bawdy, comforting. The stuffie has rolled in the deep.

*

You have to park and get out of your car to reach the stuffies at Evelyn's Drive-In, located at 2335 Main Road in Tiverton. But the view alone of the coastal pond behind the restaurant is worth the exertion. The stuffie is nice to look at too. It is presented in a wax paper lined red plastic basket. This is the first place where I've seen the lemon placed on top of the stuffie. The yellow wedge arcs over the center of the paprika and parsley dusted stuffing. This is a moist, traditional stuffie in which the breading is beautifully infused with clam flavor.

I am here with a friend from California who is tasting both her first clamcake and her first stuffie. I envy her. She asks me an intriguing question.

"Why do you write about clams? Don't lobster and

crab taste good too? Maybe even better?"

With difficulty, I remain in her company throughout the meal, but only so I can have Evelyn's justly famous grapenut pudding for dessert.

Yes, I write about clams because I love their taste. But also because, as Thomas Wentworth Higginson wrote in 1871, "I have noticed with every native Rhode Islander there is a certain tremulous tenderness of voice in speaking of then…the preeminent native of Rhode Island is the clam." This was true long before European contact. Quahogs have been central to the diet of those who live along Narragansett Bay as long as there have been people and gulls there.

*

The Quahog Emporium at 60 Brown Street in Wickford is the rare place where you can buy stuffies, quahog themed clothing and quahog jewelry all in the same place. Anyone looking for Christmas presents for me should shop nowhere else. There's even a Christmas-themed, framed Don Bousquet cartoon on the wall pretending to confuse littlenecks with Little Nicks, although I'm not sure if it's for sale (please ask). I'm glad that Don included a cocktail fork in his drawing. There are several kinds of stuffies from different sources for sale there, including from Duffy's Tavern.

I didn't make it to Duffy's itself during Stuffie Summer but visited over the winter because I'd heard such good things about its stuffies and fun atmosphere. Yes, you can find stuffies any time of the year, although the primal need for them seems to kick in with me from May to September. Little did I know I was in for the stuffie shock of my life.

There are two bars at Duffy's, the raw bar and the knotty pine paneled regular bar. I chose the latter. When the bartender handed me my stuffie it took me a moment to register what I was seeing. It was a stuffie served in a scallop shell! I tasted it to see if perhaps the stuffing contained scallops instead of clams. But it didn't. This was a Trojan Scallop stuffie. It looks like a scallop but contains an army of clams within.

I asked the bartender if the stuffies were always served that way, and she said they weren't. No one in the kitchen on that slow, snowy Sunday afternoon would tell her how they ended up with a batch of stuffies in scallop shells. "There's always a quirky twist at Duffy's," she explained. We laughed, and I enjoyed this anomaly, as unusual as a quahog pearl.

*

It is a Saturday in September and summer is ending. I stop at Skip's Dock at 1161 Succotash Road in Wakefield. My cousin, who has a beach house nearby, says Skip's has the best clamcakes. This is their last day of the season and they aren't making clamcakes, but there are stuffies. When I inquire into how the stuffies are made I receive the best possible answer from the gentleman behind the counter: "I couldn't tell you. My mother makes them." (I take a couple to go and heat them up later. Good job, Mom.)

From Skip's I head to the Matunuck Oyster Bar, 629 Succotash Road, South Kingstown. Word of the stuffies at the Matunuck Oyster Bar had reached me earlier in Stuffie Summer by way of one of my advance scouts, a friend from law school who lives in Connecticut, but who ate there while vacationing in Rhode Island. It was the first stuffie she had ever had, so she couldn't say how it compared to others, but she thought I needed to try it.

What are the odds that the last stuffie of Stuffie Summer will be the best? Well, it is. This is a place that farms oysters in the salt pond behind the patio where I'm sitting. I can't see it, but they also have a farm where they grow their own produce. The stuffie has big cubes of Italian bread from a bakery in Providence mixed with clams, chourico and peppers grown on their farm. It has a loose rather than dense stuffing. I've never felt so light after eating a stuffie; I've never lifted my cocktail fork so ravenously and easily through twenty bites of stuffie.

The owner Perry tells me that this isn't the first stuffie recipe they've used, so I know this perfection wasn't achieved without some trial and error, like the invention of the light bulb. I just hope the recipe never changes again. When Perry hears about all the stuffies I've been eating he quizzes me about my other favorites and why I like them. He tells me I should write about oysters next, and maybe I will eventually. But I have one more quahog book left in me first....

Matunuck Oyster bar is open year round, but Stuffie Summer is now closed.

*

Why did I spend a summer eating all the stuffies I humanly could? One reason is to provide a snapshot of the culinary state of my state at this moment, to determine and document how its unique food traditions are both persevering and evolving. For a moment in October I feared that some of the places I visited on my Stuffie Summer would never see another summer because of

Superstorm Sandy. I am happy to report that, despite many other losses, every place I wrote about survived. And even though the roof of the marina near my house blew off, my own roof survived its one hundred and twenty-second hurricane season.

Another reason for having a Stuffie Summer is to continue a tradition in Rhode Island not only of eating clams, but of speaking of clams in such a tone of reverence and love that those not born on our Quahog brimming Narragansett Bay want to love them too. Yes, I'm proselytizing for the Rhode Island quahog.

In case you're wondering, I actually lost weight during Stuffie Summer. I suspect this is because I made stuffies my whole meal on most of these visits, instead of an appetizer before a bigger meal.

I think I know how to enjoy clams and summer, but I met one couple at a clam shack that made me feel like a novice. They had commandeered the picnic table with the best view of the sailboat studded harbor and set it with fresh flowers and a tablecloth. It was a BYOB establishment, and they had a bottle of Sakonnet Vineyards Vidal Blanc chilling in an ice bucket. So far, the picture is as lovely as the wine glasses they were clinking together at sunset, but not altogether unique. What really sets this duo apart is the next detail. They were eating steamers. It is traditional in eating steamers to dip the clam first in hot clam broth to remove any sand and then in hot melted butter. Unfortunately the butter and broth cool off when you're making your way through a hillock of clams. This couple solved that problem by bringing their own personal invention, little sterno heaters over which they set small metal pans in which they had poured the butter and broth, which was still steaming hot when they shared the last clam. Part of me wants to go on television to pitch Stuffie Summer Travel Broth and Butter Heaters, but the other part of me just wants to thank this couple for teaching me how to live each moment of summer.

This was absolutely going to be the last time I spent a summer on a quahog seafari. But the story is not over until I spend a season savoring the clam in its most famous role of all. Sure, the connoisseur loves the clam in 'cake and stuffie, but the general public knows and loves it best among a supporting cast of potatoes and salt pork in a clear, red or creamy broth.

Coming soon. The marathon bivalve eater returns with the final installment of the Rhode Island Quahog Trilogy:

Chowder Summer: One Man Eats Rhode Island, Manhattan and New England (And Still Has Room For Oyster Crackers).

Here are two stuffie recipes, inspired by my Stuffie Summer journey. They are my original recipes, but owe much to the stuffies you have read about above.

Al's Hot Chourico Stuffie

This recipe is named for my stepfather Al, who hails from Fall River, Massachusetts, where chourico is like mother's milk. He loves clams as much as chourico, and I have seen him eat, at one meal, a heap of steamers, a bowl of clam chowder, a stuffie and fried clams.

This recipe is for two quahogs and yields four stuffed quahog shells.

2 quahogs

1 cup celery chopped

1 cup bell pepper diced

1 small onion chopped

4 tablespoons butter

1 teaspoon minced garlic

½ teaspoon cayenne pepper

¼ pound ground hot chourico

1 cup Ritz cracker crumbs

1 tablespoon chopped fresh dill

Preheat oven to 375 degrees Fahrenheit.

Cover the quahogs with an inch of water and cook in a loosely covered large pot until the shells open and the clams are cooked through. This will take about ten minutes. Discard any clams that don't open. Remove the clams from the pot with tongs and let cool. When cool enough to handle, remove the clams from the shell and mince. Separate the halves of each shell.

Brown the chourico in a frying pan for a minute or two over medium heat. Add the butter, chopped vegetables, garlic and cayenne and cook until the celery, onion and bell pepper are almost, but not quite, soft. Remove pan from heat and stir in the crumbs, minced clams and dill. Mix thoroughly. Use a tablespoon to stuff shells with the stuffing. Place on a cookie sheet, and bake in the preheated oven for 25 to 30 minutes.

Nancy's Limoncello Stuffie

This recipe is named for my mother, who loves lemon and Limoncello. There isn't any Limoncello in it, but this stuffie captures the zest and sunniness of that liqueur. Stuffies are usually served with hot sauce and lemon. It struck me during Stuffie Summer that although I encountered a lot of spicy stuffies which managed to put the hot sauce into the stuffie, I didn't encounter any that put the lemon right in the stuffie. As a result, I devised this recipe.

This recipe is for two quahogs and yields four stuffed quahog shells.

STUFFIE SUMMER

2 quahogs

1 cup celery chopped

1 small onion chopped

4 tablespoons butter

2 tablespoons of lemon zest chopped

1 teaspoon minced garlic

1 teaspoon red pepper flakes

1 cup panko bread crumbs

2 tablespoons chopped fresh parsley

Preheat oven to 375 degrees Fahrenheit.

Cover the quahogs with an inch of water and cook in a loosely covered large pot until the shells open and the clams are cooked through. This will take about ten minutes. Discard any clams that don't open. Remove the clams from the pot with tongs and let cool. When cool enough to handle, remove the clams from the shell and mince. Separate the halves of each shell.

Melt the butter in a frying pan over medium heat. Add the chopped vegetables, garlic, red pepper flakes and lemon zest and cook until the onion and celery are almost, but not quite, soft. Remove pan from heat and stir in the panko bread crumbs, minced clams and parsley. Mix thoroughly. Use a tablespoon to stuff shells with the stuffing. Place on a cookie sheet, and bake in the preheated oven for 25 to 30 minutes. Garnish with lemon wedges.

Variation: If you want a stuffie that is both lemony and hot, saute a chopped yellow banana pepper with the other vegetables.

DAVID NORTON STONE

ABOUT THE AUTHOR

David Norton Stone was born in Providence, Rhode Island. He is the author of *Trial of Honor: A Novel of a Court-Martial* and the three titles in the Rhode Island Quahog Trilogy: *Clamcake Summer, Stuffie Summer* and *Chowder Summer.* He is a graduate of Bishop Hendricken High School, Yale and The University of Connecticut School of Law.

www.ingramcontent.com/pod-product-compliance
Lightning Source LLC
Chambersburg PA
CBHW061339040426
42444CB00011B/2989